To Dad, still the smartest person I have ever known, with all the Love of a grateful son and with the only regret that he never could know my children.

Jayden's Funny Tales

"Two Dads Under the Christmas Tree"
by
Tobias Mile

✶✶✶

Illustrations
Milan Samadder

Editing consultant
Samantha Reid

1ˢᵗ Edition, September 2020

Jayden's Funny Tales

①

Two Dads Under the Christmas Tree

by

Tobias Mile

Illustrated by

Milan Samadder

TRUE COLORS LAB, PUBLISHING

Preface

*My name is Jayden. I was born on the night of December 24, 2017
in Washington, D.C. in the United States, and this is my story.
Or maybe, I should say my first story...*

***

No matter how hard I try, my memories of the first few days are jumbled, to say the least. I can only say that at some point - *I don't know how, I don't know why* - I managed to get out - *thank goodness!* - from that dark, damp tunnel in which I had been floating for about nine months.

Let's be clear: I'm not complaining, but a little fresh air after so much seclusion has never hurt anyone.

In short, I was out! And although the light was a little too bright for my liking, and someone had been shouting and fussing all throughout the process, I felt quite satisfied with myself.

Since the beginning, I think I slept a lot and, in addition to a sensation of total relaxation, I do remember many excellent bottles of milk and people of all kinds constantly fumbling with me, flipping me over like a small chicken on the grill, and the pleasant feeling of being in the clouds.

Then, suddenly, I was in a rather cozy home with soft lights and gentle whispers filling the air. Outside the window, I saw little pieces of cotton falling out of the sky and...two dads under the Christmas tree.

Month 1

My crib is absolutely soothing and I plan on spending as much time in it as I possibly can. Even the background music - *this guy Mozart* - is not bad and it helps me sleep pretty well.

And the room service is top notch. With one cry, the staff starts moving.

With two cries, one dad enters the room and the other one goes to the kitchen.

With three, I already have the bottle in my mouth.

Sometimes, even if I'm not hungry, I try to play if the "call service" works and I punctually see them jump.

In fact, I think they are a little tense. A dozen times a day, even at night, they suddenly undress me looking for a dirty viper - *that's what they say*. I don't know exactly what they do, because unfortunately, I can't see well from my position, but for a while they lift my legs up and down and never find anything.

And every time, they talk about a certain ointment to put on me, which, in my opinion, smells terribly like poop and is probably good for keeping vipers away.

Today, when I woke up, there were many people bent over me. My dads said they were friends who came to visit me. But what kind of friends were those?

They all tried to kidnap me or use me like a football! Dads were vigilant, though, and everything went well.

Well, all of it, except for the huge puke I threw up on a lady who bounced me for ten minutes straight with a stupid smile on her face.

In the end, she was no longer laughing.

Month 2

These two daddies are not half bad. I mean, they could be a little more refined, but, on balance, I'm seriously considering extending my stay here. They are very caring and attentive - *often too much* - and I try to please them by dispensing smiles and finishing all my milk, which seems to fill them with satisfaction.

Simple people.

Every time, as soon as I take the last sip, they congratulate me as if I have accomplished some extraordinary feat and they give me two or three hundred pats on the back. Obviously, almost always, this thumping makes me burp, and when this happens it's as if they'd won the lottery.

You never saw such happiness. I would like to tell them, "Guys, calm down, it was just a burp!" But I let it be. If they're happy, I'm happy.

This, however, is causing me to doubt their qualities as educators, since it is well known that doing these things is generally frowned upon, especially in public.

All in all, life goes by pretty smoothly and time flies. Yesterday I heard one of the two saying that two months have already passed and that the supply of formula is running out. He also said they had to change the nipples. Well, if milk is running out, that's a problem, but I don't understand why they want to go into surgery when I am absolutely fine with my bottle.

Strange people.

Thank goodness, one of the two just said he was going to buy milk.

That's a relief. Time for my nap.

Month 3

There was a flurry of excitement at home this morning. Dads talked about "being late," whatever that means; they came and went from my suite very agitated. After a quick feeding, strangely without too much cuddling, they tore my clothes off and plunged me into the bathtub. After the grooming, handling me with unusual "nonchalance," they dressed me up and buckled me quickly into the baby carrier, all wrapped up and ready to go to the North Pole.

So we left the house in a hurry, and after a short drive we finally came to this "doctor" who my dads had been talking about all morning long.

The man, dressed in white, lived in a white house, full of white lights, with other people also all in white. What fantasy!

At first glance, he seemed like a nice guy, but I was wrong. Initially, he smiled and was kind. He paid me compliments, and he treated me with care. Then, he started to annoy me and spite me. He twisted my legs, put a round disc of very cold metal on my chest and back, lowered my tongue with a stick and stuck spikes in my ears. Clearly, he didn't like me! Next, the traitor obliged my dads - *I say obliged since the poor guys had tears in their eyes!* - to hold me down on the exam table while he pierced my thigh with a knitting needle.

For the rest, I don't remember anything else... except for his face that I will never forget, because when I grow up I will go back to look for him!

(And when that happens, I'll take my dinosaur with me!)

Month 4

Today, for the first time, I heard my dads talking about the arrival of a certain little brother, or maybe a little sister. It happened after a phone call that left them quite disoriented. They asked me if I was also happy, and I couldn't answer them - *because the question caught me by surprise, or because I still don't actually speak.* But if I could, I'd tell them that I need to think about it. However, brother or sister, I have no intention of sharing my bed or my bottle. So if we agree on these two conditions, then yes, I'm happy. At least I will have someone around to play sophisticated games with me instead of this ridiculous "peekaboo!"

They started with this little stunt a few days ago while they were changing my diaper. My stomach didn't feel well, and Little Dad complained of a certain disaster and didn't know where to put his hands. I was a bit restless, so Big Dad, while helping with the cleaning service, started with that farce to keep me quiet. The game is simple: an adult - *not totally right in the head* - hides his face in his hands, then he pops back into the view of the baby, saying, "peekaboo!"

The problem is that if you laugh the first time, then the adult goes on for hours. Well, I laughed, it's true, but not so much for the game itself as for the fact that, after the first "peekaboo," Big Dad's face reappeared all streaked with poop.

Little Dad started laughing more than me, while the other smelled his hands and catapulted to the restroom shouting words I can't repeat.

Little Dad still laughs...

Month 5

Do you know when you wake up, in the middle of the night, and you feel peckish? Well. Ignore it and go back to sleep. I wish I had!

Instead, poor me, tonight, unable to resist, I made the usual call for room service. Immediately, Big Dad appeared at the door complaining to the other about a Dawn who was not here yet - *perhaps they were talking about the babysitter, though I could have sworn her name was Sophie.*

In the semi-darkness, I noticed that the poor fellow didn't look well and walked dragging his feet. After a few minutes, and after a horrible racket in the kitchen, Big Dad reappeared with my bottle in his hand. He lifted me up and, holding me firm in one arm, he put the bottle nipple first in my eye, then in my mouth.

So while he was savoring the thought of going back to bed, I savored the sensation of molten lead still glowing, moving down my throat. To prevent my tongue from melting, I spat everything out like a dragon and screamed at the top of my lungs. This brought Dad to reality. He jumped up and started screaming with me!

Curiously, Little Dad shot off the bed and started shouting as well. Three fools screaming in the night, each against each other.

In a moment, I found myself in the restroom, suspended on the sink with my attacker's big hand trying to fill my mouth with water. As I was about to drown I thought, "Enough milk! If I survive, I want to be weaned!"

Anyway, my tongue recovered immediately and, before I fell asleep, I got tons of kisses and a delicious warm bottle.

Month 6

"We're going to Europe!" I don't know what that means, but it sounds cool! I heard it from dads who were super excited and who argued a lot while putting their things into colorful boxes with handles. Little Dad filled two huge ones because he wanted to take along the whole house, and 92 pairs of shoes. Big Dad, rather, insisted on bringing only one. He kept repeating that he only had two hands and he didn't know how to manage me. I just hoped I wouldn't wind up in one of those boxes too!

"We flew for thirteen hours" - *so they said on arrival* - but they were only showing off because we were actually locked up all the time in a long, crowded thing called an "air plant," in which they ate, slept, and fumbled with my diapers, but they certainly did not fly.

The journey by car seemed endless and between a nap and a feeding, my daddies updated me on the stages. "Jayden, are you happy?! We are in Rome!" "Hey baby, we're in Montecarlo! Isn't that great?!" I don't know why, but they were so happy.

After many updates on our whereabouts, while I was still napping, I heard Big Dad say, "Let's take the baby in our arms to take a picture!" Little Dad pulled me out of the stroller and said, "Yes, but first we have to change him. He peed a lot." Then they exclaimed, "Jayden, can you imagine?! You're only six months old and you're already in Venice!"

So I looked around and...Oh my gosh! I couldn't believe how much I peed without even realizing it!

Month 7

My dads work in the music field. Big Dad is an orchestra conductor, Little Dad is a manager which means "Director of Everything." He is also Director of Big Dad.

Today, for the first time, I went to work with them! I attended the rehearsals of a real orchestra. So cool! The seating arrangement was outstanding. They had positioned me with the stroller between the violas and the cellos, and from there I really enjoyed it. Big Dad gestured a lot, waved a white stick and looked at everyone.

He looked at me too. Except that he smiled at me, while at times he made ugly faces to others. Anyway, he didn't beat anyone with the stick.

I liked the music very much and, during the intermission, all the musicians wanted to hold me in their arms. One of them, Jamie, also brought me to play the Timpani, two copper pots that, instead of using to make minestrone, you have to hit with two mallets.

I also received some applause because I think I did a good job. Then the rehearsal started again and, in the end, everyone congratulated my dad for my talent, because - *they said* - I was able to take a nap even in the middle of Rossini's "Thief Magpie." I don't know who this gentleman is, nor did I see what his bird stole - *since I was asleep* - but I must say that I actually do have a real talent for naps. Especially on a full stomach.

The day was fun. However, while we were leaving the rehearsal room, I cried because I thought it was a wonderful idea to take the timpani to the hotel to practice a little bit more, but my dads disagreed. You know, every great career had to overcome big obstacles in the beginning!

Month 8

What a beautiful summer in Italy! I met my Grandma, all the uncles and cousins, and a thousand other people, less nice than them, who in turn lifted me, kissed me, squeezed me, breathed in my face, tickled me and - *everyone, and I mean everyone* - touched my curls to be sure it wasn't a wig. But now - *how do you say that?* - "Home Sweet Home!"

News: I love pasta with tomato sauce, I like colorful shapes, I have four very hard little squares in my mouth, two above and two below. Yesterday I also tried to use them on Dad's arm and I think they work well since he yelled and jumped from the armchair. Another bit of news: my bassinet has become too small and they also say dangerous, because now I know how to roll over and lean over the side. Dads immediately bought a new crib for me and one for my sister - *because we found out that she is a girl!* - and they have prepared a beautiful bedroom, full of books, colors, toys and all sorts of comforts. Anyway, if they believe that I will sleep there alone, in that cage, with all those animals around watching me, they are very wrong. There is a ridiculous mouse, with ears like two vinyl records, who stares at me persistently from a shelf and for this reason I am rather uncomfortable. Yesterday they tried to leave me there, but I shouted a lot and now here I am, in their king bed.

While I pretend to sleep, I listen. One of them said that maybe it's not a good idea to let me sleep with them, but the other convinced him to let me stay by saying that I was still a baby. And after all, he had read somewhere that "Puppies never sleep alone!" What wonderful things you can learn when you read!

I love these two guys!

Month 9

Yes, I love them, but cohabitation is not always easy. I would like to sleep while they would like to watch a movie. When I want to eat at night, they want to sleep.

When I have a sudden artistic impulse and I start painting with the first thing I find in my hands - *for example, my soup* - they shout and immediately clean me and erase my Art. It seems that they want to nip in the bud all my endeavors!

Boring people.

If I put a little ball in my mouth, they shout "No! Spit it out!" If I put my fingers in certain little holes in the wall, immediately "Noo, stop it!" If I climb on the coffee table and try to pull down the full teapot, they scream - *in unison* - "Nooo! Watch out!"

If you don't know me, you might think my name is No rather than Jayden.

In short, like in all the best families, there are misunderstandings. Not to find excuses, but would you consider that I am American and they speak only Italian at home? And so fast! I'll do my best to understand. Then, please also consider all my dads' friends and colleagues and all those people we meet at the grocery store who speak to me in English with a thousand different pronunciations. I do my best to understand what they want from me, but can you see that it's a little complicated?

However, I am making mental arrangements and I'm going to give my first public speech very soon. Currently, the good thing is that I know how to cry, scream and laugh correctly in both languages.

And, to be honest, my dads always understand me.

Month 10

Today my dads invited Grandma to spend the holidays with us. What the holidays are, I do not know yet, but I will find out soon. A curiosity: while talking about her arrival with a dear friend, whom they call Aunt Vale, they explained that they would also organize the Tombola, an Italian game halfway between the raffle and Bingo, which Grandma loves very much. I also dreamed of it tonight.

In my dream, there was a white-haired gentleman, sitting aloft, in a kind of gold high chair, ready to announce the five lucky numbers for that day. In front of him, ninety cribs, each with a number and with boys and girls of all races and colors inside.

And I was there too. With each number drawn, the corresponding crib lit up, the baby was called by name and peeped out. The prize was a pair of parents - *or perhaps even a single parent* - who was randomly awarded. As soon as they discovered their winnings, they started crying or laughing, depending on their liking. Some children were happy. Others less so. A chubby and hungry child was given a skinny vegan mom and dad. Oh, my! Another, who was very squeamish about food, won two moms with four huge milk jugs, ready to nurse him without stopping. Sad for him! A little girl, who dreamed of becoming an animal rights activist, won a dad who was a butcher. She cried her eyes out!

When my number was called, I woke up suddenly and found my daddies, smiling, standing over my crib. I thought, all things considered, that went really well and...I went back to sleep, happy.

Month 11

Dads said that my sister should arrive any moment now, so I don't understand why we are going somewhere to get her. Maria Assunta: what a name! Too long and too difficult! I decided I will call her Mimì, and I hope she is nice.

On the one hand, I am curious to meet her. On the other, I hope she is not one of those troublesome girls. Dads in the last days were skyrocketing, constantly talking about the preparations for the trip and the whole house was invaded by disgusting pink dresses and bows.

During the flight, I slept a lot and I only remember I dreamed of flying. It was great! On leaving the airport there were a lot of people waiting for their loved ones, but Mimì did not show up. Then, a yellow car took us to the hotel, but even there I saw no trace of my sister. What if she changed her mind? Maybe she found a better place to go. Did we come all this way for nothing?! Where are her manners? She made me very angry. Daddies, however, did not seem to mind at all and were enjoying two pizzas in the room.

Suddenly, there was a phone call. I understood that Mimì had finally arrived, but that we had to run to the hospital. Maybe she had had an accident! Oh, no, maybe she was sick, and maybe even contagious! I knew something would go wrong! But wouldn't it be better if we stayed three?! As we ran out, I started crying loudly because I didn't want to go to the hospital and get infected. Daddies silenced me with the pacifier and then I don't remember anything else.

When I woke up there were four of us and that chick was crying nonstop!

Month 12

Here we are! I just discovered that the month I was born is back, and Little Dad does nothing but talk about Christmas decorations. Mimì is crying less now and my legs are making progress, so much so that I often feel the desire to launch them in short and fast runs. I think my dads have the same desire because, when I do, they start running too and shout confusing things, especially if I'm near the stairs that go down to the basement.

I have to say that they are often faster than me, but I'm working hard to improve my performances. In short, everyone seems super excited and there is also a lot of talk about a certain birthday party and the arrival of Grandma Assunta from Italy.

This afternoon, while I was taking a nap, the Christmas tree magically reappeared, and below it there were many colorful packages. Certainly, however, they do not contain other dads since they are too small.

Tonight, in the king bed while pretending to sleep, I heard them whispering. Grown men are definitely strange: they talked about me, the Christmas tree, Mimì, and the most beautiful gifts they had ever received. They said they were so happy. Then, suddenly, they hugged each other - *with me in the middle!* - and they started to cry.

But didn't they say they were happy? Umm...who knows with them?
Goodnight!

Dear Children and Parents,

Thank you for enjoying little Jayden's diary with me. I hope this is only the first of many funny stories that will bring you joy.

I was lucky enough to meet this beautiful family during my trip to Italy and, after learning their story, I decided that I would create something special around the adorable Jayden, who has remained in my heart ever since.

As you may have guessed, this is not only the story of a child's first year of life, but it is an Adoption story.

It is the story of an act of Love, because this is what the word "Adoption" means.

In the mysterious and complex movement of the universe, an unknown mechanism is triggered at some point that ensures the paths of several people will converge to impact each of their lives.

Somewhere in the world, there is an orphaned child. Or a couple of parents, or maybe even just a mom, or just a dad, who feel that they can't, or don't want to take care of this baby for some reason. These birth parents selflessly decide to entrust their child to others who will be able to care for him.

In another part of the world, a mom and a dad, or maybe just a mom, or maybe two moms, or two dads, have always been waiting for that child with open arms, with an open heart, with a sole intent: to give him their Love.

This is Adoption, with a capital A.

It doesn't matter where, or how, or what color or gender all these people are.

The only thing that matters is that they will be a family. They will live for each other and their lives will remain linked, inextricably, forever.

And this is Love, with a capital L.

Tobia Smile

Jayden's Funny Tales ~ Book 1

TWO DADS UNDER THE CHRISTMAS TREE

by

TOBIAS MILE

***

Published by True Colors Lab, LLC

244 Fifth Avenue, Suite C 215 - New York, N.Y. 10001

www.truecolorslab.com

For permissions contact: marketing@truecolorslab.com

Illustrated by Milan Samadder

Made in U.S.A.

ISBN: 978-1-7354108-0-7

CPSIA information can be obtained
at www.ICGtesting.com
Printed in the USA
LVHW070709030121
675534LV00002B/20